Colored Highlights

and

Drifting Shadows

~Friendship's Moments~

~Ophelia – Marie Flowers

ISBN:1511413352
ISBN-13:9781511413350

This book is dedicated to:

My dear friends
Both present
And past
Who have brought me joy,
Urged me to chase dreams,
Held me when I cried,
Stood by me through every hard day,
Taught me valued lessons
And drawn me closer to God –
I have not deserved such gracious people.
Thank you for being a part of my life.

Most importantly
This book is dedicated to God,
My dearest friend,
Who has never forsaken me,
And who has always been my guide.

My words
Fail to express
The depth of emotions
Wound in a human heart,
But God,
I ask Your grace
To try to speak Truth
In this way –
To You be the glory.

~Ophelia – Marie Flowers

Special Thanks

I couldn't have done this without my critique partners, editors, and those who took the time to encourage me to keep at this.
You all found so many mistakes and made me really think. Thank you so much for making this book what it is:

Juliet Lauser, Jonathan Garner, Camilla Uphaven, Travis Perry, Rose Williams, Nathaniel Fackler, Kimberly Perez, Hayley Jackson, Deborah Christian, and Alex Mintah.

Thank you to everyone who allowed me to quote you on friendship. Thank you for taking the time to ponder what friendship means to you, and the lessons you've learned:

Faith Woltanski, Karissa Bedford, Ellyn Eddy, Isaac Fox, Susanna Buckley, Hayley Jackson, Tori Peckham, Mirriam Neal, Elizabeth Kirkwood, Juliet Lauser, Theodora Ashcraft, Glenna Schleusener, Brendan Hanley, Travis Perry, Caleb Baker, Calista Beth, Joel Parisi, Mark Coddington, Katie Daniels, Cody Krueger, Daniel Woltanski, Stephen R. Lawhead, RSSharkey, Camilla Uphaven, and Grace Pennington.

Contents

I Wanna Be Your Friend

1/31/14 Age: 19

I wanna make a footprint in your heart,
Wanna send a smile to your soul –
Wanna touch your heart as you touch mine,
To show you the One who makes us whole.

I wanna make a sparkle in your eyes,
Wanna send a laugh to fill your day,
Wanna give a touch to show I care –
Loving you as I begin to pray.

I wanna make a hope within the pain,
Wanna give a hand in time of need,
Wanna stand by you whatever comes,
Even in those days that my heart bleeds.

I wanna make a song to lift your heart.
Wanna send a light to flood the space –
Wanna send a prayer through the night,
Whispering there's hope beyond this place.

I wanna make a memory in your mind,
Wanna leave a joy tied to my name,
Wanna give a friendship that will last,
Even though our lives won't stay the same.

I wanna make a difference in your life,
Wanna share my love (though I am small),
Wanna run with you to win the race,
Reaching Him who is our All in All.

Ecclesiastes 4:9 – 12

"Two are better than one, because they have a good reward for their toil. For if they fall, one will lift up his fellow. But woe to him who is alone when he falls and has not another to lift him up! Again, if two lie together, they keep warm, but how can one keep warm alone? And though a man might prevail against one who is alone, two will withstand him – a threefold cord is not quickly broken."

I Promise, Friend

2/18/2011 Age: 16

I promise to hear you, friend,
Whenever you need to talk.
I promise to pray for you
As you go through your Christian walk.
I promise to trust you, friend,
As you have trusted me.
I promise to guard all secrets
As best as I can see.
I promise to stand by you, friend,
No matter what befalls.
I promise to aid you as I can,
Whenever your voice calls.
I promise to love you, friend,
As a sibling close to me.
I promise I will pray for you,
Wherever you may be.
I promise to tell you, friend,
If I think you go astray.
I promise to weigh my words,
And try to bless through what I say.
I promise to show you, friend,
Friendship that endures.
I promise to be your friend,
From here to Crystal Shores.
I promise these to you, friend;
These promises I'll try to keep:
To be your friend on dry ground,
And when swimming in the deep.

It won't all be easy, friend,
But God won't make me try alone.
You will be by my side,
For in friendship we have grown.
It won't all be easy, friend,
And I ask correction when in need.
I don't always think through my words –
They often come in speed.
It won't all be easy, friend,
But may you do the same for me.
I hope you understand,
What your friendship has come to be.
It won't all be easy, friend,
But I promise you I'll try.
I'll need to ask forgiveness,
'Cause I will mess up sometimes.
Not all will stay the same, my friend,
But I'll always be your friend.
I will always remember you,
To the day this life does end.
It won't all be easy, friend,
And I can promise I will fail.
I know I'll try again though,
For you are wind within my sail.

"We are shaped by our friends; the ones who build us up, the ones that understand when we're down, the ones who offer not just a shoulder to cry on, but an ear to listen and a mouth to communicate an understanding."
~Karissa Bedford

A Prayer For You

1/10/12 Age: 17

Dear friend, I'm asking, "Why?"
I hear your pain and start to cry.
You make me sigh these days.
Why do you hurt? I sob this way.

Dear friend, I hurt so bad.
The pain you feel makes me so sad.
I love within my heart.
I feel inside what tears apart.

May God do what He wills.
I pray for you His peace that fills.
Never lose your hope.
He longs for you to more than cope.

I don't know what to say.
I simply close my eyes and pray.
"Dear God, oh please, reach down.
Please, oh please, don't let her drown."

"Heal her, Lord, today.
She's breaking now in every way.
Help her trust in You.
Remind us that You'll see her through."

May God reach you tonight.
I pray you're blessed with Heaven's light.
Even though the skies may fall,
God is here – He answers your call.

"In my experience my closest friends are the ones who saw me at my worst and stayed by my side, not because they were still attracted to me, but because they loved me. "True love is this, that while we were still sinners, Christ died for us," after all."
~Isaac Fox

I'm Not Okay

4/22/14 Age: 19

That unguarded moment
When my shield
Drops –
And there you are.
"Are you okay?"
You saw my frown
And the way my shoulders sagged
'Cause I thought
No one was watching...
While at the same time, I was wishing
Someone would notice.
"I'm fine. Just tired."
My practiced smile falls into place
As I list
All the reasons why
I'm fine
Just
A little tired right now.
Those entangled words
Slip past my lips.
Part truth –
Oh,
But mostly lie.
I think you believe me;
If you didn't
You'd probably try to probe
Deeper.
You're good at it,
But I never give you the chance.
See,

We all have *those* words.
Those words
We hide behind
At the times
We're the lowest.
What are *your* words?
Mine are these,
Clear as day,
"Okay"
"Doing fine"
"It's been a busy week" −
Yet you don't see them
For what they really are.
But that's my fault.
I've gotten good at pretending.
Heh,
So good
You wouldn't even know
Half the time
That I'm repeating in my head,
"It's okay.
I'm okay.
It's okay.
I'm okay."
Over and over
To stop my other thoughts
From sinking me
Deeper than I want to go.
I don't often let my guard slip
Low enough for you to see...
But
Despite all this...
I want you
To chase behind the words,

"I'm fine."
To see
If the words are real
Or
If they're an empty shield.
Please...
I need you...
But right now
All I do is smile and laugh
While we dance around
The truth...
I'm not okay.
I'm ready
To give up
Hiding
If I have to...
But please,
If I really have to open up,
Will you
Please stay with me?

"Every friend I have ever known has taught me something about the character of God. Most have done so without knowing it."
~Susanna Rose Buckley

They Are Inspirational

10/13/11 Age: 16

They hurt, Lord, and I don't know what to say.
They are bought by You too,
And it hurts me to hear their pains.

They laugh, Lord, and I don't know how they smile.
They live in awe of You,
And I wonder if I could do the same.

They give, Lord,
And I don't know where it comes from.
They are amazing in so many ways
And I wish I could express admiration better.

They trust, Lord, and I don't know how they do so.
They have a positive outlook,
And I love who they are for it.

They are, Lord,
An inspiration I don't know how to explain.
They shine You in everything,
And I pray someday to have faith like that.

1 John 4:7 – 8

"Beloved, let us love one another, for love is from God, and whoever loves has been born of God and knows God. Anyone who does not love does not know God, because God is love."

I Won't Pretend

11/16/11 Age: 16

I can pretend that it isn't true.
I could turn away from the pain consuming you.
Not care.
Not call.
Not serve.
Just stall.

I can pretend that I didn't know.
I could turn away while you stumble and sink low.
Not help.
Not hope.
Not show.
Just cope.

I can pretend that I didn't hear.
I could turn away while misleading words leer.
Not teach.
Not give.
Not bless.
Just live.

I can pretend that it isn't so.
I could turn away while your unending cries grow.
Not reach.
Not try.
Not love.
Just sigh.

But I won't pretend that I do not see.
Though my heart may cry, God will help me be:
His hands.
His voice.
His feet.
This choice.

"Take a minute and make someone's day. Tell your friend you love them. Chat with the person you've been meaning to chat with for a while, but haven't gotten around to it. Compliment people. Tell a stranger you like their band/geeky t-shirt. Start a conversation and ask sincere questions. Listen when people tell you important things about themselves. Hug your friends. Don't hesitate. It's amazing how little things can bless people (and you)."

~ Hayley Jackson

A Friend

7/12/2010 Age: 15

A friend is someone special;
A true one you can't buy.
A friend is very special,
And here are reasons why.
When you really want to chatter
About lots of funny stuff,
A friend can laugh right with you
Till you cannot breathe enough.
When you have a funny story,
Or something else you want to tell;
A good friend listens closely;
A good friend listens well.
When with some you are more proper,
And quiet, and polite;
With a friend you can be silly,
And they think it's quite all right.

When you're feeling very lonely,
A friend can make your day.
A laugh and a smile can take your frown away.
When something makes you sad,
And you feel like you will cry,
A friend can sit beside you
And needn't know the reasons why.
When you really need a prayer,
A friend can lift one high.
A friend can be there for you
When the devil screams a lie.
When you need to know the truth,
Or an opinion of something,

A friend can be a help
In the perspective that they bring.
When you need some extra help,
A friend can be right there.
A friend can support you,
And you know they'll take great care.
So you see that friends are special,
Each in their different ways.
I'm glad God gave us friendship
To brighten up our days.

"Friendship is sacred and divine. This is not a human term. Jesus called us friends, because He laid down His life for us. Friendship is a love-bond so strong that it empties us so that the other person may be filled."
~Tori Peckham

Please Speak Through Me

10/30/11 Age: 16

Why me, God?
Why do You call me to speak?
I am so afraid
I'll say the wrong words.
What if
I only make things worse?

Why me, God?
Why can't someone else do this?
There are others
Who could say it better.
Why can't
You choose one wiser than I?

Why me, God?
Why do You let them tear my heart?
I feel their pain
And I am sobbing inside.
Why do
They hurt so much?

Why me, God?
Why did You call me to this?
There is no way
I can do this without You.
Please speak
Your words through me.

To Trust
6/4/2010 Age: 15

To trust is to give a part of you away.
It means you believe what someone does say.
To trust is to believe that they are true,
But sometimes people your trust misuse.

Trust is not something you can buy.
It is easily broken with a lie.
Trust you build, and trust you break.
Be careful whose trust you take.

People sometimes break our trust,
But I know my God is just.

"There is a reason for every person who has ever walked into my life. Sometimes they only stay for a short season. I've learned to treasure the moments rather than worry about the future."
~Anonymous

When I Lost You

7/29/14 Age: 19

Sometimes I think
I let myself
Love you too much.
It wasn't hard –
You saw me for who I was
And somehow still cared about me.
We saw eye to eye on a lot of things
And the things we didn't
We could still discuss together.
Much laughter was found
In silly late nights –
Much strengthening was found
In honest conversations.
When one of us fell
We were there to come alongside,
And comfort was found
In prayer and understanding.
I wanted us to be friends forever.
We were good friends...

Until it broke.

Words were said –
Just like that
Things became...
Complicated,
Churning,
Twisted...
And it fell apart.
We pulled back,

Back,
Back –
Until we snapped the ties.
Stopped talking.
Stopped searching each other out.
Stopped being there.
It was almost surreal
Watching that friendship die.
The panic of losing you
Seemed unbearable in the beginning.
One of the worst pains
I've ever felt...
You were an important part of my life.
But things change.

This doesn't seem fixable –
We've both moved on
With lines drawn to keep our distance.
Walls are up
And I don't know how to break them...
Or even if I want to anymore.
I have to face the reality
That I've truly lost you.
Time has passed and yet
There are still some days I smile
And remember you,
Or wince
Because memories are too overwhelming.
Sometimes I think
I let myself
Love you too much
But then again,
I believe it was worth it –
Good friends are.

And So I Prayed
6/27/2010 Age: 15

You were sitting all alone,
And I didn't know what to do –
So I prayed for you.
You were looking very down,
But I didn't know what to say,
So I closed my eyes and prayed.
My heart was saying, "Talk!"
But my head said,"I cannot!
I don't know what to say,
Not a glimmer of a thought."
When I write, the words come quickly.
To you, they just will not.
I should have still been friendly.
My fear I should have fought.
You are quite fun to be with,
You are funny and listen well.
I didn't know how to cheer you up,
So to my knees I fell.

"Two friends… There are stronger forces on earth perhaps, but few as tenacious and enduring as the bond between true friends."
~ An excerpt from the book,
Merlin
by Stephen R. Lawhead

Growing Up

10/1/12 Age: 17

Growing up used to be forever away –
At least that's what I thought.
I'd play, write, laugh, pretend,
While dreaming of the day when I'd be grown.
That would be a good day.

I'd be grown up
And you, my friend, would be with me, forever.

Now growing up is almost here –
And it's tinged with a quiet ache.
I'll work hard, earn, save,
But that's not what hurts me.
It's not hard work I fear.

I'm growing up
And I can't take you with me, forever.

I have seen you growing, too –
A pride of friendship's affection.
I've encouraged, shared, prayed –
Glad to see you striving onward.
Now you're grown up too.

We're growing up
And it comes time to step away for a bit.

Our bonds are not going to break –
We're closer than that.
I'm brave, quiet, nodding,

But inside I'm sad.
I never thought growing up would mean letting go.

We're growing up
But I will keep you in my heart,
Forever.

"In my experience, there are only a very few things that a friendship needs to become something gold: trust, and common denominators. If you have these with any one person, you can have a solid friendship."
~Mirriam Neal,
author of the novel,
Monster

My Dear Friend

10/12/2010 Age: 15

I try to think what I'd do without you.
You bring joy to my life; I hope you know this is true.
I don't often express this verbally to you,
But it wouldn't come out like this will do.
You are understanding when I have something to say,
That means a lot to me in every way.
I've told you secrets that I know you won't share.
I know if I need you, you'll be there.
You mean so much, I can't explain.
You're like a rainbow, when I feel like rain.
When God gave me you, He saw just what I'd need.
I think that was such a wonderful deed!
I know you're not perfect, but neither am I.
You mean a lot to me; I hope you know why.
You make me laugh like no one else can do.
I wanted to say that, "I'm missing you!"

"Friends are good. They're good for making me cry, laugh, think, and move when I can't make myself."
~Juliet Lauser

Friend, You Are

11/22/2010 Age: 15

Friend, you are a rainbow;
A sparkle in the rain.
You are so amusing when we act insane.
Friend, you are the sunshine;
The brightness and the fun.
You can bring excitement before each day is done.
Friend, you are a stream;
Laughing through your way.
You always amuse me by the teasing things you say.
Friend, you are a breeze;
Steady, quiet when there's need.
Willing to listen, and sometimes to lead.
Friend, you are a snowflake;
Unique all your own.
In this respect you are not alone.
Friend, you are a sunrise;
Bringing a beautiful day.
Spreading smiles in all that you do and say.
Friend, you are lightning;
Flashing sudden, flaring bright.
Showing joy and understanding in words and sight.
Friend, you are special;
May this day be special too.
I pray that God leads you in whatever you do.

Why?

12/15/11 Age: 16

Why, why, *why*, do you hurt?
I know it's not for me to know.
Why, why, *why,* does God test you like this?
I know, somehow, it must be for His glory.
Why, why, *why*, do I hurt?
I know it's because I care.
Why, why *why*?
I've cried for you.
I've prayed for you.
I've questioned almighty God with the word:
"*Why?*"
He's saying, "No," or, "Wait."
I'm praying it is
"Wait."
It's just so hard...
But I have no reason to complain,
When what I feel
Is only a shadow of your hurt.
How come you can be stronger than me?
But,
Your sicknesses aren't bogging me
Into a depressing blah.
Because,
You all make me smile.
I am blessed by your words.
I am encouraged by your trust.
I am praying harder.
I am learning better how to give my burdens to God.
I thought you should know.

Not Meant To Say Goodbye

8/5/13 Age: 18

I don't believe we're meant to say goodbye
Or to feel the stinging ache when we do.
And I don't believe that we were made to die –
That's why it hurts to say goodbye to you.

I don't believe we're meant to say goodbye.
It's harder the closer that we grew.
But I do believe someday we'll know why,
And we'll dance along God's shores in sunset hue.

In Heaven, one day we will know why,
And understand the things we never knew.
In Heaven, we will never hurt nor cry,
Or wonder at the things we have gone through.

In Heaven, there will be no need to cry –
No pain that our moments were too few.
In Heaven, there will be no teary eyes –
We'll be with our God, who died to make us new!

James 1:19 – 20

"Know this, my beloved brothers: let every person be quick to hear, slow to speak, slow to anger; for the anger of man does not produce the righteousness of God."

"I've seen God do some pretty impossible things. I know and believe He can and will mend broken relationships."
~Faith Marie Woltanski

Broken Trust

3/12/12 Age: 17

The words I said
Weren't what I meant them
To be.
They came from within
But I should not
Have said them.
I was afraid
And I took it out on you,
My friend.

I said I'm sorry –
You said I'm forgiven,
But it's not the same.
Trust is broken,
And it will never be
Quite the same.
That hurts
Badly.

Still, God is in control.
I'll wait on Him
And His timing
To heal this wound.

"Friendship takes effort, time, patience and love. So make the effort to take time. And have the patience to truly love."
~RSSharkey

Only One You, My Friend

4/10/12 Age: 17

In all of this world,
There's only one of you.
No one quite the same,
Who does the things you do.

You let me ramble at you,
And don't mind when I'm insane.
You laugh when I'm befuddled,
And will explain to me again.

You make my world better,
Just by being there.
I try to make you smile,
'Cause I want you to see I care.

You always make me smile,
And for you I've cried.
I lift you up in prayers,
And am filled with joy inside.

Someday I hope, dear friend,
You will know that it is true,
And really understand,
How much I do love you.

Trusting God With You

8/13/12 Age: 17

You hurt, and it's making me ache.
I'm wondering if I've made a mistake.
Pounding Heaven's door for your sake,
Crying until I start to break.

You hurt, and it's making me cry,
Screaming at Heaven's door, "God, why?"
Feeling like my hope is dry.
Longing for my faith to fly.

You hurt, and there's nothing I can do.
I feel my heart tearing in two,
Yet I am trusting God with You.
I know He'll fix and make things new.

"*The most important thing I've learned is* **enjoy the time you have with the people and places you take for granted**. *Because in the literal blink of an eye, they can be taken away.*"
~Caleb Baker

Lost Friend

10/25/12 Age: 17

Because I don't understand
And I don't see why.
Oh, my heart is breaking,
And I start to cry.

Where did I mess up?
Could I have done more?
Why did this have to happen?
Oh, you shut the door.

And I look back now,
On the things unsaid.
Hearing them as echoes,
Bouncing in my head.

I want to go back,
Loving one more time.
And explain what you meant,
To this heart of mine.

It hurts so much,
A churning ache.
I want to have it back,
No matter what it takes.

But God still is good,
And He's holding fast.
My only wish now,
Was that it could last.

Now it's gone,
That friendship dear –
But it'll never truly pass,
For in my mind it's clear.

"Sometimes, you just feel like you can't help your online friends. Everyone has felt like that at one time or another; some more than others. After all, what can you do? You're words on a screen. You can't stop bad things from happening to the ones you love, because you're on opposite sides of the country.

That's not true. Not entirely, anyway. There are things you can do or say. You might not be able to protect them physically, but you can support them emotionally."
~Theodora Ashcraft,
author of the book
Of Whispers and Wanderings

To My Internet Friends

10/30/12 Age: 17

I never could have imagined
How much I would love you,
Friend.
I never would have thought
That a love like this could form,
Or that I would so fiercely defend you,
Pray for you,
Cry for you,
And rejoice with you.
I never could have imagined it.
Especially since...
This love formed without ever seeing you face to face.

In the beginning
I never considered
How much you could make me hurt –
How often I would cry for you...
I never considered
How hard you could make me laugh –
How often I would gasp for breath at your words...
I never considered
How blessed you could make me feel –
How often I would close my eyes
And praise God for your friendship.
I never considered
How knowing you would change me.

When I hear your happiness
I can't help but rejoice.
When you share a triumph
I'm ready to declare it to the world.
You're my friend;
It doesn't really matter that
You're thousands of miles away –
Except when I want to take you by the hands
And spin around with excitement.

When I hear your pain
My heart breaks in two.
When you ask me to listen
I cry to God to give me something to say.
You're my friend;
It doesn't really matter that
You're thousands of miles way –
Except when I want to wrap my arms around you
And hug your hurts away.

There are ways I'll never be the same
Because you touched my life.
Thank you for
Trusting me with your heartaches and questions,
Blessing me with your contagious excitement,
Reminding me to trust in God's promises,
Being there to pray and listen,
And for taking the time to be a true friend.

I never could have imagined
How much I would love you,
Friend...
And I think I'm only truly *beginning* to understand
What that kind of love truly means.

The People In My Life

12/2/2010 Age: 15

Lord, thank You for the people in my life.
They help me through turmoil, and fears, and strife.
Lord, thank You so much for the people I know.
They put life in perspective and help me to grow.
Lord, thank You so much for the people around me.
They surely don't realize what a help they can be.
Lord, thank You so much for the people I love.
They are a blessing, a gift from above.
Lord, thank You so much for the people I see.
They are special, to You and to me.
Lord, thank You so much for these people who share.
It is a blessing just to know that they care.
Lord, thank You so much for these people who give
A testament of how each Christian should live.
Lord, thank You so much for these people of You.
They inspire me with all that they do.

Let's Go Fly

11/28/12 Age: 17

Oh friend, let's go soar,
Looking for something more;
Let's go swim in the deep
Where hope and laughter meet.
Let's go find forgotten things,
Let's go soar on glossy wings;
Let's touch the sky.
You and I
Gonna fly.

Oh friend, let's go sing
Remembering the joy it brings.
Let's go dance in the field,
Forgetting darkness life can yield.
Let's go find mystery's song,
Let's find out where we belong.
Let's sing again
Now and then
Wonderin'.

"The most important lessons I've learned about friendships is knowing how to hear each other, and helping the other feel more real than just a simple reflection in the mirror."
~Karissa Bedford

Hidden Heartaches

12/17/12 Age: 17

When I close my eyes
And the tears come,
Sometimes I try not to let them fall
Because you are there –
With me, as you often are,
Ready to listen if I need it.
One word that's not quite right,
And I know you'll be asking me questions.
Questions I don't want to answer.

Sometimes it seems easier to smile
And launch into a funny story
Than to try and explain the tangle of emotions
That is me.
If I can keep your well-meaning questions at bay
Then I can stay under control.
But if you ask the right question
I may end up
Leaking my heart all over.
Right now, it seems safer to laugh
Than to bare my heart.

Would you really understand
If I laid it all out before you?
Let's be honest here –
We're not little kids anymore
And our life problems are a whole lot bigger.
Scarier.
Darker.
Burying them seems to be the better option.
Better than hurting you.

I keep telling myself I'm looking out for you.
That's why I don't tell you what's going on.
These are my burdens
And I don't want to see the pain in your eyes
When you discover how deep they are.
I'm just keeping you safe...
At least, that's what I tell myself.

Some days I let you in farther than I mean to.
Instantly, you're there with comfort.
You remind me of God's goodness
And His never-failing love.
But even as you say the words,
I see the pain in your eyes.
I don't want you to hurt for me...
Because I don't feel I'm worthy of it.

Why do you love me so?
Why do you hold me until you ache?
I don't think I'm worthwhile,
But you say it enough that I almost believe it.
I'm not worthy of it
But I think we're both weary of hearing me say it.

Maybe tomorrow when you ask
I won't say I'm just fine.
Maybe tomorrow, I'll tell you the truth.
Some days, you do hear it
And some days, I keep it back.
I don't ever want to be the reason you cry...
But I'm learning to let you in.

Alone, Surrounded

12/24/12 Age: 17

Do you see me?
I feel as if, to you, I'm invisible,
Even though we stand in the same room.
For a moment, would you look at me?
If only for an instant, could you come close
And show you care?
You can be there,
Right beside me, talking now
And yet, I feel so alone.
I'm surrounded on all sides.
You're in the room with me,
But somehow you're not
With me —
Not in the way I wish you were.

Just because you are *near* me
Doesn't mean you haven't left me feeling alone.
For a moment, could you take the time
And talk with me?
Not talk at me about inconsequential things,
But talk to me —
Talk to me about how life is going for us
Or ways we've grown in Christ this year.
I wish you would.
You have left me feeling this strange kind of lonely —
The kind of lonely that comes from being ignored
And, at times, blown off.
I don't begrudge you for it
I only wish the word "together"
Meant more than standing in the same room.

"You have to work at friendship. You can't just sit back and wait for friends to show up – and once you have friends, you need to make the effort to spend time with them."
~Glenna Schleusener

I Miss You

1/25/13 Age: 18

Oh, some days I miss you.
Do you think of me at all?
Oh, some days I wish you
    Would give me a call.

Oh, some days I miss you.
    We grew up and away.
Oh, some days I miss you
    And wish for those days.

Oh, some days I miss you.
    I've tried to let go.
Oh, some days I wish you
    Somehow could know.

Oh, some days I miss you.
    Life keeps moving on.
Oh, someday I know you
    May truly be gone.

"There are so many people that you can genuinely help, don't stick with the people who just want to manipulate you."
~Brendan Hanley

Open Smiles, Trampled Heart

2/5/13 Age: 18

You're not who I thought you'd be
When I first met you.
Did you honestly think
I'd never notice?
You laughed with me
With open smiles,
But when I needed you
You weren't there.
You turned your back
When my world fell in –
Avoiding me
When you should have been the first one
There to comfort me.

Now you laugh with me again
While inside I am screaming my pain.
When you look at me
I want to tell you just what I think.
Don't you see what you've done?
Don't you understand
You trampled my heart
Into a wet mass on the floor?
No.
I don't believe you do...
And I can't work up the courage
To tell you.
Part of me clings to my memories
Of back when we were
Best friends.

I once thought
I could fix things between us.
I once thought
I could make things all right.
Now I see
Things are beyond repair.
Our ties are snapped
And there is no fixing it.
A few times, I've tried
But there's no changing what is
Or going back to what was.

Now here I stand with open smiles
And a trampled heart.

"You find out who your most precious friends are in your hour of greatest need. Those who stick with you and believe in you when others speak evil of you – they are worth more than gold."
~Travis Perry,
author of the book,
Medieval Mars

I'm Not Letting You Go

2/5/13 Age: 18

I hear your words of aching
And the pain in your tone.
Your life is falling around you –
So much that weighs you down.
When you wake up in the morning
Your biggest hope is to make it through the day
Without breaking down...
Or at least
Not where people can see it.
You think no one cares
And you're too afraid to let someone know
How deep your pain really is.
On the outside, you are mostly smiles
But I saw you hesitate just a bit when I asked
'How are you today?'
You told me you were fine
But something inside told me not to believe you.
Why won't you let me in?
I don't know how to help
But I am willing to try
If only you'd let me.

This fight you are in,
It is between you and yourself.
You keep dragging at who you are
And never letting yourself take pride
In even the smallest accomplishment.
So often I just want to shake you,
To tell you over and over and over
"You are loved!"

"You matter!"
"You matter to *me*!"
Any time I say it though
You just give a little laugh
And show me the smile
That doesn't reach your eyes.
I want to know about you –
Know *you* –
Even though I know it will break my heart.
I give you permission to cry,
To let it all out
And tell me just what you think
About this messed up world.
You are my friend.
You may not believe you even deserve a friend
But I'm not going anywhere,
So you might as well get used to it.

When you fall,
Don't dive into yourself,
Into the darkness you feel.
Instead, run to the Throne Room of Heaven,
Then tell me, and I'll join you there.
Because I am your friend
And I am never letting go.

"The Bible speaks of there being a 'time for everything'... Sometimes, the time calls for 'iron sharpening iron', through relationship. Sometimes, the time is one of letting go.

There are seasons for friendship. Sometimes a person enters your life, by God's hand, so that you can pour into them. And when the time is complete, they move on.

God 'binds' people together in relationship by His Holy Spirit. When a door closes on a friendship, it will hurt; but it will be okay. The ending does not mean there is no love between people. It means that the season for the friendship that existed has changed. Like the seasons of Earth – winter, spring, summer, fall – change. Life changes things."
~Camilla Cruz Uphaven

Not Mine To Keep

2/11/13 Age: 18

You know the saying,
"This person means the world to me,"?
There are people in my life
Who fit that category well.
But two of them I feel I'm losing...

One friend will soon go away for a year,
Then probably to Africa shortly after...
Where I may never see her again.
She's got a passion for it, and a love in her voice
That brings me to tears
And makes me so very proud of her.
She's not afraid to go into the most dangerous places
To bring Your word to those in need.
She's going after Your will with a passion
That is resounding with Your glory.
God, I know you're going to do great things
In her life.
She's got a heart that loves so deeply
And a zeal to serve the least of these.
But oh God, I ache at the thought of letting her go.
I am struggling with...
Giving her back to you.

My other friend
May be leaving and I don't know how long...
She won't tell me why.
I'm aching, deep, deep...
Her, I never considered
Losing.

This is so unexpected.
I assumed she was constant
But perhaps now I will lose her.
What is wrong?
Why is this happening, God?
Am I too dependent on her?
Is that why You ask her to leave?
My head is muzzy from all the crying I've done.
She promised to tell me in time.
I know she's not mine to keep, but letting go
Seems more than I can bear.

God, why would you do this?
I see you doing great things in their lives
But I'm not ready to let them go...
I want to curl up and cry some more
Because this hurts so much.
They aren't mine;
I keep feeling that every time I pray.
They are Yours...
Yet, You placed them in my life
And interlaced my heart with theirs.
I've said it before – they are Your gift to me.
Now I feel You're taking them back.

True, I know You're not fully taking them away.
But their interaction with me will be different.
A difference that I don't know how to deal with.
Still, I trust there is a purpose.
I know that You are good.
I believe that You will use this to deepen my love
For them
And for You.
So may Thy will be done.

You've Gone On Ahead

8/18/14 Age: 19

Oh, you've gone ahead to Glory,
While I am left below.
I still think of you daily
And wish I could tell you so.

Oh, you've gone ahead to Zion –
What a legacy you leave.
There's rejoicing at your story,
Even though our hearts still grieve.

Oh, you've gone ahead to Heaven –
Yes, your life is now complete.
You can see the Savior's glory,
Where His love and mercy meet.

Oh, you've gone ahead to Jesus –
What joy must now be yours,
As you play beside our Savior
And dance along His shores.

"Friendship hurts. It hurts to love, to risk rejection. But it is only when we take the risk that we find the beauty they hold."
~Calista Beth

Love Hurts

3/5/13 Age: 18

Love hurts.
I look at your tears,
Listen to your heartaches,
And I long to help you make sense of it all.
You've got a world of worry pressing in,
With so many concerns,
Questions and hurts
Striving for your attention.
I love you, friend,
No matter what you're going though.
I'm going to be here
Even when love hurts.

This love hurts,
But I love you anyways.
Your crying breaks my heart
But part of me knew, when I began to love you,
That this would happen.
This is a true showing of my love –
It's evident in the way I long to heal this
And in the way I pray for you today.
Oh friend,
Remember you are loved
Despite your pains.

Love hurts.
I watch your anger,
See you building walls
And wish I could shake some sense into you.
You've got a lot to think about,
With so many disappointments,
Questions, and frustrations to deal with,
And you're trying to fix them alone.
I love you, friend,
No matter how fiercely you shout me down.
I'm going to be here
Even when love hurts.

This love hurts,
But I love you anyway.
Your anger makes me cringe
But part of me knew when I began to love you
That this could happen.
This is a true showing of my love –
It's evident in the way you wound me
And in the way I pray for you today.
Oh friend,
Remember you are loved
Despite your deepest struggles.

Love hurts.
I've watched you growing,
Walked down many dark paths by your side,
And been there with you for years.
You've started to step into the world,
With all your interest,
Longings, and dreams you hope for
And long to achieve.
I love you, friend,
But I realize I have to step back to give you room.
I'm going to be here
Even when love hurts.

This love hurts,
But I love you anyways.
Your leaving makes me sad
But part of me knew when I began to love you
That this would happen.
This is a true showing of my love –
It's evident in the fact I'm letting you go
And in the fact I pray God takes you wherever.
Oh friend,
Remember you are loved
Despite the distance between us.

Love hurts.
I see you fading...
I cry, realizing our friendship is different,
And I know you're shifting out of my life.
You've grown apart from me,
With a steadiness,
Quietness, and certainty that I didn't want to see,
And now I have to accept.
I love you friend,
Even though we're not the same as we once were.
I'm going to be here.
Even when love hurts.

This love hurts,
But I love you anyways.
Your going leaves me wondering
If there was anything I could have done to stop it,
But part of me knew when I began to love you
That this could happen.
This is a true showing of my love –
It's evident in the way you still touch my heart
And in the way I never stop praying for you.
Oh friend,
Remember you are loved
No matter what.

Come Back To The Savior

8/17/14 Age: 19

Friend,
I see you straying –
Walking thin lines on tiptoe
As if you can stand in both worlds.
You pull your hands in and out
Of the fire
And slowly
Your fingers are showing the signs.
Painful,
Cracked,
Blisters rising on them.
You are forever wearing gloves,
Hiding your once-beautiful hands
Out of shame.
I tried to hold your hand the other day
Like we used to
But you jerked away
Not once meeting my searching eyes.
Then I truly knew
How bad it had become.
I tried to tell you how I care
And understand
But you told me you're fine
And hurried away.

I've got scars too,
Dear one.
Scars from when I played with the world,
And felt the fires lick my hands.
The flames seemed almost fun,

They dulled the pain in my heart,
Promising me I would find happiness in the heat.
Weakness would be burned away,
And I'd be free to do as I desired –
But it only crippled me,
Left me empty.
Even when I tried to back away,
The scars stung, crying
That I had nowhere else to turn.

Ah, but that's where Jesus found me.
He took away my scars.
But the memories remain,
Reminding me what He saved me from.

You tell yourself you can change,
"I can stop."
"Oh, I won't go any farther." –
But that is dangerous.
The calling world will pull you in
Until you lose your hope,
Until they break you.
You know the truth, friend –
Don't leave it to chase after pleasure.
You have the greatest joy, friend –
Don't leave it behind to play with the world.
It will burn you,
Scar you,
And leave you alone.
Trust me,
I've been down that path.
Come back to your First Love.
Trust in His forgiving grace.
No matter how deep your burns

He can mend them –
If you repent
And rest again on Him.
Friend,
Come back to The Savior
And find healing in His arms.

"Friendship is being available to listen to your friend's struggles and support them through whatever may happen."
~Joel Parisi,
author of the book,
Shadow Play

You Don't Have To Pretend

3/11/13 Age: 18

You can share the truth.
You do not have to hide.
I know that you are breaking.
I know... that you have lied.

You can stop the laughter.
You do not need to act.
I know that there is bleakness,
And oh, your heart is cracked.

You can let the tears fall.
You do not need to smile.
I know you're not okay.
And have not been for a while.

You can say what's hurting.
You do not need to shrug.
I know that you are tired,
Like this – a beat up rug.

You can tear the walls down.
You do not need to run.
I know that pain is screaming,
And the dark – it took the sun.

You can drop that pseudo–smile.
You can stop this play–pretend.
I know that you are hurting,
But know, I love you, friend.

"*People change in all different ways. Sometimes even friendships that seemed so close and unbreakable just dissolve over time. You enter a new phase of life and realize the other person did too, and you're farther apart now, because you're different people now. And even if you think you still retain that part of you that could connect with them, they seem to have shed it or buried it.*

But I trust that in eternity we will all be who we really are -- the sum of all that we ever have been. And none of those good parts of us – and none of those friendships -- will be lost."
~Ellyn Eddy

My Friend Forever

3/20/13 Age: 18

"Let's be friends."
Ah, those childish words we said
When we were young.
I didn't know much about friendship,
But you played with me
And I with you
So of course we were meant to be close.
You needed someone to dream with you,
And I needed someone to dare me to try,
And so we learned to be that for each other –
Though I don't think we thought of it that way
When we were young.
We'd be best friends forever,
Because of course, friendship to a child
Is a promise of forever.

"There's something I want to tell you."
I'm not sure how many times
We said those words to each other.
As we got older, being friends meant more
Than simple games
And general interest.
We talked about life and all the things we'd do
When we grew up.
We told each other secrets no one else knew
And prayed for each other when our worlds fell in.
We had shared so many memories,
Both good and bad,
And been together for forever
I assumed... that you'd never leave.

"I'll write you and call you!"
That's what you said
The day I moved away.
At first we wrote almost every week
About the fun things we'd done,
And remembering old times...
But one
By
One... the letters got shorter and shorter
And it took longer and longer
For us to send them.
Finally... they just stopped.
It's not that we had a real reason,
But somehow you and I got too busy
And we lost track of the time.
In that way, our friendship slowly disappeared
To only a fond memory.

"I'll never forget you."
Those are the words I whisper
As I lie in bed at night and think about you.
I've got new friends now
Who are as dear to me as you.
We laugh and dream and do many of the same things
You and I did together.
It's the little things that bring you to mind:
A book with your favorite creature,
A tree that looks much like the one we used to climb,
A food I always thought was gross
And teased you for liking...
Sometimes I try to tell others about you,
And often they listen nicely
But then comes the question,
"So when did you last talk?"

And I realize how very long it's been
Since I spoke with you.
You'll never see this, but I want you to know –
I don't think I can ever replace you as my friend
Only gain others to stand in my heart
Beside you.
To me, being friends really did mean
Forever
Because memories never fade.

It's Not The Same

5/17/13 Age: 18

You were
Once here,
But not the same way now.
I want
Things fixed
But I don't know how.

Not your
Fault, friend –
Neither is it mine.
But I
Won't say
Everything is fine.

Do you
Hear it?
That I miss you so?
I don't
Get why,
Friend, you had to go.

So I
Watch you –
And tell you random things.
But I
Don't say
How much silence stings.

You are
Still here,
But it's not the same.
And so
I keep
Playing "I'm okay" games.

Laugh here,
Smile there,
Telling you of life,
But you're
Busy now,
So I hide the inner strife.

My hurts
Seem small,
So I share just fun.
Perhaps I'll
Cheer you,
Before our talk is done.

I won't
Tell you
Exactly how I feel.
You have
Bigger things,
With which you have to deal.

I will
Be fine.
It will be okay.
I still
Trust you,
But I'm careful what I say.

For right
Now, though,
I wish that I could share,
All the
Life things,
And know that you are there.

It's not
Your fault –
You never were to blame.
I am
Learning
That things don't stay the same.

"Sometimes God allows friendships to dissipate, or distance to occur, so as to draw you closer to Him. Sometimes we depend on others more than Him, and that displeases Him. We should make sure that our relationships are not taking HIS place in our lives. If they do, they have become idols.

Trust God, He will show you the steps you need to take. He will give you wisdom, discernment, comfort, and hope for every day of sorrow, loneliness, hopelessness, or trial along the journey HE has for you."
~Camilla Cruz Uphaven

God First

5/21/13 Age: 18

You are my friend;
With me every day.
I laugh with you –
Pretend you'll never go away.

I hear your advice,
Sharing my heart.
Going to you first,
When my world falls apart.

We go through days –
Sharing everything.
I want to suppress
The changes time brings.

I share with you truth –
With you I am real.
You calm my heart
When hurt's all I feel.

You become very dear
As time goes on.
I realize I fear
One day you'll be gone.

Stubbornly though,
I try to pretend
That it won't change,
The way we are friends.

A prick in my heart
Warns you've become first –
Now before God,
And my spirit's thirst.

I try to withhold
The place where you stand.
You're held in my heart,
With tight–fisted hands.

God gave you to me –
Meant to be mine.
You're not *really* first.
Everything's fine.

So He takes you away,
Telling me it is best.
But I doubt at the time,
And cry at the test.

Then He reminds me,
He's second to none;
The God who died,
So I could be won.

Finally I can see,
What I did not before.
Though your love was true,
I let you block the door.

You became my reliance,
I could not do without.
I let what I felt,
Shade inside and out.

I should have gone to Him,
Before I did you.
I should have trusted
Instead of blundering through.

He patiently shows
What needs to change.
And works in my life
To help me rearrange.

Now with this lesson,
I'm trying to be
A good friend to you,
But keeping God first in me.

"Some people don't understand internet friendships. I do. I have them. They bless me. Because I am isolated and far away from my own homeland, they are a treasure for me.
I know that Jesus is all-sufficient for me. I know to be careful because my and their perspective is a narrow one based on what one allows to be seen online. It isn't necessarily a true and FULL perspective of one's weakness, strength, temper, need, etc....
I also know this: We can touch each other's lives in amazing ways even from afar, even without ever meeting one another in person.
Especially through prayer."
~Camilla Cruz Uphaven

Internet Friends

10/7/13 Age: 18

Keyboards click,
Words spin out.
Promises made
In midst of doubt.

Tell me now
I don't know you.
We could hide
But that's not true.

Never met
But know a lot.
Through simple letters,
Smiles. Dots.

Who I am
Is what I've said.
What you know
Is what you've read...

Who I am
Is what I've shared.
What you know,
Is how I've cared...

Who I am
Is what I write.
What you know,
Is beyond sight...

Who you are
Is how you care.
What I know
Is what you share...

Who you are
Is what you say.
What I know,
Is how you play...

Who you are
Is what you tell.
What I know,
Is when you fell...

Who we are
Is what we give.
What we know
Is how we live.

Simple codes
In smiles and dreams.
Tangled hurts
That break the seams.

Keyboards click,
Each shared hope.
Learn to laugh,
And learn to cope.

Trusted help,
Certain friend.
Promised days,
Beyond life's end.

Friends apart
But friends the same.
Known through words,
And each by name.

"Human beings were made for relationship, relationship with God and relationship with man."
~Brendan Hanley

I Know Enough

11/18/13 Age: 18

I know enough...

I know enough love for you
That inward heartache is a familiar companion.
I know enough love for you
That "protect" and "help"
Pound demanding in my head.
I know enough love for you
That feeling powerless is a part of me.
I know enough love for you
That jealousy is something I'm relearning to deal with.
I know enough love for you
That not understanding is... twisting pain.
I know enough love for you
That many of your pains interlink with mine.
I know enough...
That some days I wish I didn't...
Because knowing your dark struggles
Isn't the same as having light to fight them...
And I'm a broken warrior myself.
I know enough love for you
That part of me breaks into pieces
Every time I let my heart lean a little closer.
But hey, that's part of who I am.

I know enough love for you
That it doesn't matter what we're doing,
So long as it's hanging out.
I know enough love for you
That making you truly smile makes my day.

I know enough love for you
That the very thought of us changing hurts.
I know enough love for you
That I would do anything to be a better friend.
I know enough...
That most days I'm glad I do...
Because being your friend through this bit of life
Is a blessing I'm so grateful God gave.
And I need you as a friend
As much as you seem to want me.
I know enough love for you
That part of me focuses only on tomorrows
Where you and I are forever close.
May God grant us wisdom
To continue to bless each other's lives.

"It takes work, time, a humble heart, and resilience to make and maintain friendship."
~Camilla Cruz Uphaven

Lost In Silence
11/22/13 Age: 18

I'd rather be silent than expose myself to you.
I'm probably being stupid.
"Get over it!" Self mocks me.
You don't need to know how I'm feeling.
These emotions... they'll blow over, given time...
So I'll stay quiet.
I'll close up.
I'll smile and pretend I'm doing okay.
Better to pretend than to live that again.
We both know something happened –
Now we tiptoe on glass shards
That cut slivers on our feet
While pretending the glass never was broken...
You broke it.
I broke it.
We knocked it over together
But
Neither of us wants to admit it.
"My fault. My fault. All of this is my fault,"
Those words sing–song, laughing in my head.
This guilt is mine, but I'll hide that from you too –
No need for you to see
How warped my thinking has become.
The thought of talking this out with you terrifies me.
Still, it's what I want the most...
Yet I bury the possibility under layers –
Layers of, "It's not that important."
"I should deal with it myself."
"It wouldn't fix anything, even if I tried."
But I can't take it anymore.

I close down thoughts.
Shut them down. Go silent.
Not real silent –
But the kind of silent that never brushes past,
"Yeah, today was fine,"
To the truth –
I don't know how to tell you
What hurts.

You and I, we're still friends,
But the tension roars just below the surface.
"You hurt me!" Cries the betrayed voice in my head.
Then,
"No... I'm just being stupid..."
"The fact that I can't let this go
Shows how poor a friend I am."
We both know something is wrong
But walking on glass shards
Seems safer than cutting open the real problem.
Whose fault is it?
My fault?
Yours?
In reality it's both,
But this silence has even bound that truth.
We go through the motions like everything's okay
While underneath
We're pulling farther and farther apart.
What went wrong? I'm still not sure.
Yeah, maybe asking would help...
But I can't risk that pain.
Not again.

Then one day
A little crack. A misplaced word, a meaningless jibe
And suddenly, the landslide breaks.
Floods of hurt,
Confusion,
Longing,
Missing,
Not knowing –
All of this swirls in chaotic wind.
"But why didn't you say –"
"I didn't think you'd understand –"
"I felt alone –"
"I wanted you here –"
"Why did you –"
"Because I thought I'd lose you."
The words flow free, exposing all the tangled strings.
We tied the knots together
When we doubted each other's care.
We pulled back
When all we really wanted was to be held closer...
We both thought the damage done
Was solely in our hands.
Our feelings twist but we smooth things out bit by bit;
Apologies, promises of honesty
Give weight to our discussion.
In the end we're wiser than we were
And stronger friends in many ways.
Now we know...
Talking it out is painful,
But not as painful as pressing it down.
Honesty hurts, but it's worth it...
Because I never want to lose you, my friend,
To silence.

"I know it hurts. I know it's hard. When someone concocts and spreads lies about you, it hurts. When someone you thought was your friend suddenly stops speaking to you, it hurts. And sometimes, it seems like the only course of action is to stay angry, and to hold a grudge against them for a very long time.

Forgiving and loving the people that hurt you is probably one of the hardest things to bring yourself to do. After all, the natural response is to become angry. To feel indignant, hurt, and betrayed. But when you wholeheartedly forgive those people, and tell them so, you are set free from that prison of bitterness! Though you may feel ashamed for a while, in the end, you will feel much better – free from the burden of hate that you carried. It truly will set you free."
~Theodora Ashcraft
author of the book
Of Whispers and Wanderings

Just Tell Me

11/28/13 Age: 18

Oh, just tell me what you're hiding.
Bare the heart you'll never show.
Let me hold you back from sliding
To the darkness deep below.

Fuel the fire that you're burning.
Send the blade down to my heart.
Try to tell me what is hurting
Instead of throwing every dart.

Break the ice that keeps on cracking.
Stop pretending things are fine.
Please just tell me where I'm lacking –
Take the blow and cross the line.

Loose the shadows from their binding.
Don't re–bury what you found.
Say the words you keep rewinding
Though you've never made a sound.

Scream the anger you've been keeping.
Dash the glass against the stone.
Release all of your weeping
And the pain that makes you moan.

If you leave, tell me you're going –
Not trail away as fading mists.
This is something that's worth knowing,
Though inside the knife still twists.

Face the urge you keep on quelling.
Take that first step if you must.
But do not make me keep on dwelling
If I ever held your trust...

"*Even though love may fail to be returned, we still love. Even when friendships are hard and you may not see the point of continuing them, we love through the pain. It's not easy, its not enjoyable, but when you come out on the other side you find your bond is that much stronger.*"
~Faith Marie Woltanski

Change

12/11/13 Age: 18

How can I be so happy
And yet still feel an ache?
I smile at the laughter,
Yet wince as something breaks.

Days are filled with laughter
And nights are filled with dreams.
I've found as life keeps going
That things aren't as they seem.

Words can be misspoken
And even friends can change.
I'll hold tight to the memories,
The good, the bad, the strange.

Life is never simple
And change is a part of life.
I wish that I could fix things,
And strip away the strife.

Words can bring a smile
Or words can tear a heart.
I pray that God will mend
The things we drove apart.

We can stand in silence
Or we can learn to speak.
Honesty is costly
But worth the time to seek.

Hearts held once the closest
Can shift away in time.
But many are worth keeping,
If we'd take the steps to climb.

"I need my friends like I need the air. They are the life–blood that flows through my veins."
~ Mark Coddington

Parts Of Me

12/11/13 Age: 18

Parts of us
Live in the little cracks and spaces
Of each other's hearts.
We live in the memories
Of those who interact with us –
For good or for bad, or for not much at all,
We impact them.

You impact me...
Do you know how seeing your name makes me smile?
Do you know
How much I value you?
Do you know how I long to help when you need it?
Do you know
How the thought of your hurt pierces my heart?

Perhaps you know in part
But you can never see the way I do...
Sometimes I wish you could see a moment's glimpse
Of what I see when I see you.
You –
Little pieces of you
Live inside my memories and the lessons I've learned
Because of you.
Sometimes I wonder how long I'll stay
Within your memories...
Will you remember what we were as friends
When a decade or two slips by us
And things change as surely as the snow melts?
Will you?

Even better question –
Will I?
Will I remember the friends that shaped my life
And the hours I spent in pain
Because I loved them so much?
Will I remember the promises I made
And feel a jolt of happiness
At the memories of this year?
I wonder, as I often do,
What I will think of now in twenty years or so.
Will I see things I didn't before?
Will I still think I made the right choices,
Or will I wince at how naive I was?

Tiptoe around with me
And let's explore the days passed
And the hopes we have for the future.
Stand with me and remember
How our friendship has shaped our lives.
Life is crazy,
And oh, how things change,
But I hold on to this every time fear prickles me:
There is a God who stands outside of time
And He placed people with me
For each season of my life...
No matter what happens,
We were together for a reason.
The best thing for me to do is kneel in surrender
And pray that He uses me to impact those in my life
With His ever present love
For as long as He gives us time.

Your Friendship

11/13/2010 Age: 15

I've known you for so very long,
I hope our friendship's ever strong.
You are a trustworthy and loyal friend.
I hope our friendship never ends.
I can totally have fun with you.
I really hope that you do, too.
You are special, fun, and really great.
As a friend you are first rate.
I really want to stay in touch,
I really want to stay in touch,
Your friendship means so very much.
Goodbye for now, dear friend of mine.
I hope your life for God will shine.

"True friends are very scarce. We have a great many acquaintances and sometimes we call them friends, and so misuse the noble word 'friendship.' Peradventure in some after-day of adversity when these so-called friends have looked out for their own interests and left us to do the best we can for ourselves, that word friendship may come back to us with sad and sorrowful associations.
The friend in need is the friend indeed, and such friends I say again, are scarce. When thou hast found such a man, and proved the sincerity of his friendship; when he has been faithful to thy father and to thee, grapple him to thyself with hooks of steel and never let him go."
~Excerpt from a sermon
by Charles H. Spurgeon, entitled,
'The Best Friend'

Walking In Friendship

1/5/14 Age: 19

Another year,
Another mile –
Come walk with me,
You make me smile.
A year gone by,
A year walked through –
Time passed on
With me and you.

Look at then,
Look at now.
So much has changed.
It's beautiful how
In times of joy,
In times of pain –
You've been there
Through every gain.

In struggles hard,
In struggles deep,
We stood our ground,
Though things were steep.
With God before,
With God beside,
He's grown us both
With grace inside.

A time to laugh,
A time to cry.
We stand together –
That's you and I.
A way to learn,
A help to grow –
You've blessed me much,
I hope you know.

Each quiet time,
Each quiet choice –
A friendship's trust
Within our voice.
A single step,
A single way,
We walk together –
And kneel to pray.

A friend to trust,
A friend to seek,
And one who stays,
When I fall, weak.
Oh ever safe,
Oh ever found,
As friendship grows,
On strongest ground.

A hand to clasp,
A hand to hold,
And side by side
To walk forth bold.
As days go on,
As days go past –
My prayer is this:
Our friendship lasts.

So blessed to get,
So blessed to give –
Friendship's strength
Each day we live.
One to love,
One to defend,
And ever stay with
My dear friend.

1 Corinthians 13:4-7

"Love is patient and kind; love does not envy or boast; it is not arrogant or rude. It does not insist on its own way; it is not irritable or resentful; it does not rejoice at wrongdoing, but rejoices with the truth. Love bears all things, believes all things, hopes all things, endures all things."

Let Me Near

1/7/14 Age: 19

Know this:
I meant the things I said.
Know this:
I'll walk through times of dread.
'Cause here and now,
I'm by your side,
Just tell me
How you feel inside.

I don't
Know what I should do,
But I won't
Ever give up on you.
It can hurt
But I'll never leave.
Right now,
Just trust that and believe.

I wish
Somehow, to do more.
It aches
When you cry down on the floor.
But your hurt
Won't drive me away;
I promise you
I am here to stay.

Tell me
What it is you want.
I don't like
When things get all taut.
I'll try
And I know you will,
To walk up
Every bump and hill.

I need
To know what to do.
I need
To show I care for you.
So please
Tell me if you can
And I'll pray
To somehow see God's plan.

Some days
I don't understand,
And I feel
Pain goes hand in hand,
But I've seen
Friendship that I need,
So I'll trust
That God can always lead.

It's Hard To Stand

9/5/2010 Age: 15

It's hard to stand for what I believe,
When I know it is fun if I just go to see.
It's hard to stand, and not go along.
When they ask, the pull is very strong.
It's hard to stand and not go with the rest.
May I say no, and do what's best.
It's hard to stand, when I know they'll have fun.
They'll have a day to play and run.
It's hard to stand, and just say no.
In the back of my mind, I still want to go.
It's hard to stand, when I hear inside,
"Why won't you go? Are you so full of pride?"
It's hard to stand for what I know is right,
When it seems like more fun to go, not to fight.
It's hard to stand, but I know that I must.
God is my strength. In Him, I will trust.

"Love isn't as complicated or as simple as you think it should be. It's not something you can just write off as non-existent or non-applicable. And it's not something you can escape from. Not on this world."
~An excerpt from the book,
Superhero of the Day
by Katie Lynn Daniels

Looking For Perfection

6/1/2010 Age: 15

We're looking for perfection that we will never find.
We are only human, and in our sin confined.
You're saying,
"Someone hurt me – didn't ask me what I thought."
But did you ever stop to think that maybe they forgot?
You're saying,
"They said something that I didn't like at all."
Remember we are human and subject to the fall.
You're saying,
"I don't like this – it isn't my own way."
Remember that everyone can't always have their say.
The always perfect people,
I assure you, are not here.
And never will you find them,
Though you search both far and near.
There will always be somebody
With whom you can't agree,
But here, now in this broken world,
That's how it has to be.
For the only perfect human
That ever walked on earth,
Was Jesus Christ my Savior,
Who was perfect from His birth.

I'll Still Love You

1/26/14 Age: 19

Oh, you break me.
You've fallen again.
Now you say you're sorry,
For you tore my heart within.

Yet I'll love you,
No matter what.
Even when I'm aching,
And fierce feels the cut.

Yes, you hurt me –
I'll still let you near.
Knowing that it's aching,
But won't run in fear.

Still, I'll love you,
Precious friend of mine.
Caring ever for you
When things are not so fine.

Your pain hurts me,
But of course I will stay.
Bowing under heartache
That lessens as I pray.

Yes, I'll love you,
I'll love you still.
Even when it's hurting,
I'll stay. I will.

Proverbs 27:9

*"Oil and perfume make the heart glad,
and the sweetness of a friend comes from his
earnest counsel."*

Proverbs 27:17

*"Iron sharpens iron,
and one man sharpens another."*

Changing Friendship

2/7/14 Age: 19

"Side by side, friends forever,"
Least, that's what we said.
"Here for you, oh whenever;
We'll walk through any dread."

Here an' there, making stories –
Least, that's how we were.
Silliness, fading worries,
Time passed as a blur.

Hand in hand, always teasin',
Least, 'twas for a time.
Goofiness, loss of reason,
Partnering in crime.

In an' out, always smiling,
Least, that's how it seemed.
Heal the pain as it's piling,
Calming when we screamed.

Scene by scene, we are moving,
Least, I see that now.
Strengthening, and improving,
Though things change, somehow.

Step by step, things are a'changing,
Least, I finally see.
Life has done some rearranging;
But you're still a part of me.

"It's okay to remember...
It's okay to move on.
I will not keep hiding from the memories –
I will cherish them.
Life goes on – so do I."
~ZA

Holding On To Memories

2/7/14 Age: 19

Sometimes
I miss you so much.
The monster keeps curling in my chest
And I can't stop gasping through the sobs.
I'll be fine until...
Until I see something that reminds me of you,
Or think of something that would've made you laugh,
Or wonder what you're doing right now...
Then it's like someone is squeezing my throat
And it's all I can do not to cry.
Pull the covers up,
Shake until it's over.
Wash my face and greet people with a smile,
Like nothing is wrong –
That is a simple routine.
No one need know how sick I feel
As I acknowledge I have to let go...
Growing up does that to people sometimes...
It did it to us.
No going back now.
Is this what having a friend torn away feels like?
Does it always involve so much aching?
I torture myself listening to music
That brings to mind scenes from our friendship,
Or remembering all our jokes and stories
We created on late night whims.
I do this
And think back...
Back to all the times I laughed until I couldn't breathe,
Cried until I was exhausted,

All the times we were together
And I told you everything I dreamed about.
Some might say,
"Move on, forget – friendships don't stay the same."
But I don't let go of those I care about –
Not if I can help it.
Memories are all I have now,
And even though they hurt,
They bring great peace...
We were good friends, you and I.
Great friends.
Friends who tried to understand
Through every high and low we faced.
Friends who cared
No matter how much things hurt.
Friends who listened to every detail
And laughed with genuine joy.
Friends who shaped each other for the better,
And left footprints within our hearts.
Even in these life changes
The memories I hold of you remind me of that,
Always.

Thank You, Friend

2/9/14 Age: 19

Friend, I want to thank you
For being here for me.
Life has felt quite messy,
But still your love I see.

Friend, I want to thank you
For all the times you stayed.
In all the very hard times
I know that you have prayed.

Friend, I want to thank you
For all the times you shared.
Times in life are lonely,
But always, you have cared.

Friend, I want to thank you
For lending me a hand.
You have proven precious
As I walk life's dreary land.

Friend, I want to thank you
For pushing me to dream.
Words of love uplifting
To hopes I'd never seen.

Friend, I want to thank you
For causing me to smile –
For all our conversations
Of silliness and style.

Friend, I want to thank you
For being joy of mine.
Knowing I can trust you
Shows true friendship's sign.

Friend, I want to thank you
For blessing me today.
Know, whatever happens,
You're in my heart to stay.

When We Said Goodbye

4/24/14 Age: 19

I didn't think we'd say goodbye
Until that day came.
I didn't dream friendship could die –
We played the blame game.
I shrank to question why
And now it's not the same
Again.

And I wonder where I went wrong.
Wonder why I wasn't strong.
Wonder where you took my song
When we said
Goodbye.

I didn't think we'd say "it's best"
Until that choice came.
I didn't dream I'd ever rest
Without your smile's aim.
Now to pass life's test
And not sink with blame
Again.

And I wonder what I should do.
This world's so strange without you,
And I could say it isn't true
But I'm too tired
To lie.

I didn't think we'd say goodbye
And I hold the blame.
I didn't dream how hard I'd cry
When saying your name.
Still I question why
This pain came
Again.

I guess it's time to let go.
Time to face the final blow.
Time to realize that I know
This is for
The best.

I still
Wonder where I went wrong.
Wonder why I wasn't strong.
Wonder where you took my song
When we said
Goodbye.

"*A true friend is someone who stands up for you when no one else will. They help you become the person you want to be, in spite of the flaws that keep you stuck. They listen and understand, and will tell you the truth when you need to hear it. They remind you of God's grace and forgiveness even when you make the same mistake again and again. They respect your boundaries, values, and property as if they were their own. They stand with you through the battle of life. That is a true friend.*"

~Cody Krueger

Wounds

4/27/14 Age: 19

Ah, friend,
You'd never know, looking at me,
How broken I am.
I'm a sliver of glass
Shattered from a mirror.
I reflect what you expect me to be.
I smile now
But tonight I'll scream into my hands,
Silently begging
The pain to go away.
Silently pleading
With God
To ease my agony
Or take me Home.
Home with Him
Away from this pain.
The inward pain.
The outward pain.
The pain in my heart
And the pain I bring myself.

For now
I press it all down deep
And tell myself
Everything is really just...
Fine.
I'm fine.
Fine.
Fine.
Fine.

I'm really just fine.
But the darkness presses at my mind
And all my thoughts find focus
In a longing
To dull my pain.
I can dull the pain
With a moment of a little more...

You smile at me
Never guessing
How the wounds in my soul
Are leaking to stain my skin...
My broken skin...
You'd never guess
How often the longing overtakes me
And I'm left to deal with the deadening ache
As I break myself
Again.
It started out small
But I found too late
That I'd fed a growing monster.
Now it claws my heart to shreds
As I do what I don't want,
Yet have to continue,
For fear of the pressure
Constricting my mind.

Fear keeps me
From seeking you out
To help me.
Fear
And shame.
I hate myself.
Hate the things I do.

Hate what I see when I see myself...
Wondering for the thousandth time
How long would our friendship stand
If you knew.
Please, I need to know...
Would you love me still,
Even if you knew the truth?
That thought mocks me
A thousand different ways
As I hide.

I long for you to reach me,
Hold me close,
And stay
Even when I try to push you back
By telling you I'm fine.
If you could see
The truth
Would you stay with me?
I need you to know
I'm not okay
But that doesn't mean
I'm beyond hope.
My skin is broken –
So is my heart –
But still I cling to God,
Begging Him to send me
Someone
To love me
Beyond my weakness.
Can I trust you?
Can I trust you to see
Behind the scars
To my troubled heart?

If you saw my struggles
Would you...
Still see *me*?
Please, please,
Don't leave me
Alone.

"We find ourselves in others and others within us, but the relationship is so much deeper than being a mirror. It's a bond that mimics family, a sense of belonging, a sense of worth, and a worthy cause to live – and continue living – as we grow in our friendships."
~Karissa Bedford

Through The Years

5/1/14 Age: 19

I'll always remember
Those long walks
In the creek
You and I had almost every summer.
The heat was all around us,
Mosquitoes pestering our every move,
Despite the spray,
But we pressed on down that little creek
In the woods.
More than one year
I broke a flip flop when we walked through mud
And you'd just laugh at me
'Cause I'd done it again.
It was you and me –
Splashing through the shallow water
And talking about life.
Heh,
We had a lot of questions back then,
But I realize now how much simpler it was,
When I was fifteen and you were thirteen.
School,
Family,
Sleepover plans –
Mostly, our conversations stuck to those topics.
The "future" seemed so far away –
And yet it was creeping closer,
Faster than we ever dreamed.

I'll always remember
The time I sat alone in your yard

Under a tree
Praying and crying.
Other friends were over,
But I'd gone outside alone.
My heart was heavy with a prayer
And all I could do was cry –
Hurting under another's pain
That I saw no way of relieving.
I was crouched over,
And though I heard you come close
I didn't look to see at first.
You didn't know what was wrong
And I don't think I even told you at the time,
But I still remember...
You hugging me.
I can't begin to explain what it meant to me
Knowing you were there.

I'll always remember
When I really started pursuing
Writing.
You were a writer,
Full of ideas and creatures
And I wanted to write something you'd like.
You might've been younger
But I really looked up to you –
I wanted you to be proud of me.
We talked about dragons,
Our crazy night-dreams,
And how experiences worked into stories –
Stories that we discarded as new ideas
Overtook us,
And seemed like the more exciting story
To write.

We wrote in code
And gave each other notes every week –
It was like a secret
That only we could share in.
We were writers at the stage
Where we thought all our writing was good,
And we didn't wonder too often
About being cliché.
When I wrote poems specifically for you
I hoped it'd somehow express
How special you are to me
And how deep my trust runs.
Ah,
You started my passion to write.

I'll always remember
Those nights we talked past midnight
About every little thing
In our lives.
The later it was
The sillier we became,
Yet often our talks would take a serious tone
As we whispered of our dreams,
Fears,
And questions.
I never doubted
I could trust you
So I rambled about everything,
Knowing you'd guard my words
As carefully as I protected yours.
I could see how things were changing,
As new friends came into our lives,
But I knew that you were *mine* to keep –
Even when shallow fears of losing you

Fought inside my head,
You reminded me that we were friends for a reason:
You weren't going without me.

I'll always remember
What our years of friendship have taught me.
I'm nineteen now
And you're seventeen.
So much has changed
But most of it for the better.
We've done a lot of growing up
These last few years.
We're both busier now
But we still find the time to hang out,
To be together.
I treasure those times
All the more
Now...
See,
I've been thinking again
About how much you mean to me
And all the precious memories
That have you in them.
Thank you
For making me laugh
(So hard I almost choke),
And making me cry
('cause I know you care enough to see my tears).
Thank you
For being a wonderful friend to me.
No matter where growing up takes us
Know that I treasure you
More than I could ever say.

"Even if you live miles and miles apart, you can still make a difference. Words are stronger than you realize, whether they're prayers or reminders. The saying 'sticks and stones may break my bones but words will never hurt me' is a lie.

*The fact is, words **do** hurt. And just as they can hurt, they can heal, too."*
~Theodora Ashcraft
author of the book
Of Whispers and Wanderings

It Presses Down

6/3/14 Age: 19

I stopped breathing
A long,
Long
Time ago...
Back when things became too much
And I curled over
Under all the weight...

Now
I just sob.

How am I to breathe
When those I love
Are
In such pain?
Tell me
Why do their tears
Send
Such agony to my heart?

Some days
I handle life well...
Seemingly.
Other days
I bow over
Mentally screaming,
Help.
Please
Help.

I'm *trying*
But it's never enough.
Never enough.
Oh God,
It's never
Enough.
I can't dam back
The flood of fear
Or turn back the tide
Of this pain.
My friends
Hurt
And I don't know what to do.

Please...
I feel so alone
With all my thoughts
Pressing
Inward
To smother me...
Will You please
Send my heart
Relief?
God...
Do you hear me?
I need You
Now.

Oh God,
I can't do this on my own!
I've never felt...
So helpless.
My words of comfort
Are so *useless*

Compared to what I know
You can send.
Please...
Don't leave my friends
Alone.
Please...
Send hope –
To each of us.

Loyalty To Jealousy

10/18/2010 Age: 15

I love with strength and loyalty,
But sometimes it turns to jealousy.
I see someone who means so much;
I don't want to share their smile or touch.
I give my heart with love so strong.
I want to feel like I belong.
I love so deeply from my heart.
I want to be the best from the start.
I pray to let this feeling go.
Oh God help me, true love to show.

Jealousy

6/5/14 Age: 19

This Jealousy
Wonders if you'll stay
Or if new friends
Will pull you away.
It corners me
With thoughts that play
With a mind
That so quickly strays.

This Jealousy
Is a whimpered sigh –
Tells me friendships
Are meant to die.
Colors worry
With every lie
As I listen
And start to cry.

This Jealousy,
Is a bear inside –
Born from love
But lanced in pride –
It threatens me
As I try to hide
Away from hurt
On this sloping slide.

This Jealousy
Is a jagged knife
Pressing down

And dulling life.
Whispering
There's no end to strife,
Or the off-key tune
Playing on this fife.

This Jealousy
Is a creature wild;
Holds tight fists
Like a wayward child –
Leans down deep
With emotions piled,
Words unsaid
And tightness riled.

This Jealousy
Is all too real,
It churns inside
With all I feel.
It takes my joys
As a thief would steal,
And all I see
Is this selfish deal.

This Jealousy
Scrapes in my chest,
Screams with pain
As it steals my rest.
It never sleeps
Though I try my best
To drive it down
Through all that's stressed.

This Jealousy
Is a dangerous thing.
Creeping anger
With a painful sting.
Flies around
On powerful wings –
With a grating laugh –
It ever sings.

This Jealousy
Pulls me to the ground,
As I let my fears
Deafen every sound.
Never once
Can true trust abound
When I doubt your love
Will stay around.

This Jealousy
Is on the attack.
It digs at me,
Clinging to my back.
Veers our words
Way off track
As I tell you why
My trust you lack.

This Jealousy
Is a hard pressed foe,
With no fool-proof way
To make it slow.
But I'll try,
Not to let it grow –
For it shall die

As love I show.

This Jealousy
Is a choice I make,
When I feed my fear
'Till I start to shake.
So I bend my knee
Praying God will break
Its hold on me
No matter what the stake.

Sharing A Friend

11/30/2010 Age: 15

When I have to share you, I find it to be tough.
I find myself afraid our friendship isn't strong enough.
Will you cease to love me? Is she more fun than I?
This feeling's such a tangle, I feel that I may cry.
I've known you for so long, and she is still so new.
I get afraid sometimes, afraid of losing you.
I've never had to share you before.
This sharing is new, and my fear all the more.
You are compared to her and I'm jealous deep inside.
My thoughts are whirling, and my feelings are wide.
It's not that I don't like her; she reminds me of you.
The thing that I fear is what our friendship will do.
But clearly you show me your friendship is true.
You're still my good friend,
And there's room for her, too.
You are a person who can be friends with more.
I need to just trust you; that's what friendship is for.

"One of the most important things I personally have learned about friendships is that you don't have to be super-close or have known someone super-long to share important things (struggles, hopes, fears, doubts, etc.) with them. When you know that person loves God and you have the amount of trust needed to know they aren't going to laugh at you or go and blab to everyone they meet, that's all you require.

*All too often I am held back from sharing and letting people into my life because I didn't think they cared or I thought we had to be on some really deep level of friendship to share important things. But that's not true. That's just a lie that keeps you from ever opening up. Christian friends, **real** Christian friends, already share a level of closeness with you that other people can't. We are connected by the love of Jesus, and in that love, you have the freedom to love them unconditionally, just as they have the freedom to love you unconditionally. So it won't scare them off when I share my deep-seated repetitive sin. It will produce love and prayer, which is what I need to bring healing anyway."*
~Daniel Woltanski

Unexpected Friendship
7/29/14 Age: 19

I guess I would say
You were unexpected –
Unexpected in the most wonderful way.
I mean, who could have expected
Someone like you?
I went into last summer without a clue;
No idea what it'd be like,
Or what type of people
I might meet along the way.
Off on an adventure
Without a friend there beside me.
Just...
Wanting to serve and have a fun time.
Braced in the knowledge
That all summer fun comes to an end
And often, sadly,
So do those friendships.

Then you came.
Oh,
You came and poured your life
Into mine.
With no half measures,
You came and became
My dear friend.

At first
I didn't know what to expect from you.
To be honest
I'd already started settling into a routine,

Mentally,
And you seemed too sudden
For my already-overwhelmed self.
Ha,
But that feeling didn't last long.
Nope.
Not long at all.
We were meant to be friends.

I wish I could pinpoint
When we became close
But it was kind of a blur
Of laughter
And long talks
Stretching into days
And weeks,
And months.
You understood both sides of me –
The silly,
Excitable,
Sometimes hyper side –
As well as the
Wondering,
Deeper,
Longing-to-help side.
Being with you was an adventure
Of the best kind.
As we got to know each other more
You played with me,
Laughed with me...
Cried with me,
And held on tight,
Especially when it hurt.

I can't imagine what the summer would have been
Without you.
So many of my favorite memories
Have you.
Oh, the many times
I hugged you goodnight,
After a long day...
Oh, the many times we went out witnessing
Telling others about God's sacrificial love –
Joyously sharing
What He had done in our lives.
Oh, the many times
We watched the sunrise
And sang of the wonder of our Creator.
Oh, the time we shared a snack
While painting our nails after an impulse buy
Just for the fun of it all.
Oh, the many times
We got excited over silly things
And just laughed
And laughed
Together.

I love that
When we come together again
It's natural,
Normal,
And happily crazy.
I love how we play off of each other
And understand the weirdest things.
I love how we can be silly together
Easily;
Skipping hand in hand
And talking in strange inside jokes.

I love listening to music with you,
Talking for hours about the important things
In our lives.
How things are changing
And the changes we're looking towards.
I love that you challenge me
To do better –
Your sweet encouragement
Means the world to me.

I found a friendship
With you
That I thank God for –
Oh I'm so grateful
Our friendship has lasted
Beyond that summer.
God knew how much I needed you then
And how much I need you now.
He knew how well we could be there for each other,
The lessons we'd learn,
And the things we'd face
Hand in hand.
Thank you
For understanding,
Caring,
Listening,
And letting me do the same for you.
Thank you for trusting me
And being someone trustworthy.
Thank you for being such a precious friend.

From Christian to Christian
Life contains only
Temporary goodbyes –

That's what I remember when I miss you so.
I love you, sister.

*"There are a thousand beautiful joys in friendship –
one of them is the delight of laughing together."*
~ZA

Laughing

9/11/13 Age: 18

Shoulders shaking,
Head thrown back,
Laughing
Until I'm gasping
And my sides ache
From trying to be quieter –
That's the kind of laughing I like.

A contented feeling,
A wide smile –
Listening
As a friend laughs
At something I said,
And hearing their amusement, their joy –
That's the kind of laughing I like.

Crazy looks
And silly faces,
Shaking
As silent laughter builds
And nothing need be said
To grow each other's giggles –
That's the kind of laughing I like.

The stifled sound
Of teasing
Escaping
Late at night
When we should be in bed
But we're having too much fun –

That's the kind of laughing I like.

Mutual enjoyment
Of a shared joke,
Snickering
At things no one else could get.
Repeating the nonsense
Until both can't breathe –
That's the kind of laughing I like.

Being together
To laugh despite the day,
Understanding
How to make the other smile
In what we find funny
When we share our stories –
That's the kind of laughing I like.

It's the laughter of true friendship.

The Gift I Never Sent

8/11/14 Age: 19

I find it in the closet
Labeled with your name,
A gift I always meant to share
Before that moment came.
A funny little present
I never got to send –
In the simpler time before...
Before I lost you, friend.

I laugh at the inscription,
Scrawled with silly lines,
So many inside jokes are there
In squiggle marks and signs.
Oh, many messy letters
We wrote with silly flair,
About the things we reached for,
And how we really cared.

I find myself the music
We used to listen to,
And let the melodies take me back,
To times of me and you.
It makes me wince a little
To remember times before,
'Cause it will never be the same,
For we have shut that door.

I close the gift up sadly
And store it back away.
Perhaps I'll take it out again
A few years from today.
Though our friendship ended
So many things remind
That you were very dear to me –
I'm glad our paths entwined.

"My friends have always been there – lifelines to help anchor when life is tossing me around, voices of reason and hope when I lose my head, and ones trusted enough to sit and cry with as well as laugh hysterically with at three in the morning. My dearest friends can always make me laugh."
~Elizabeth Kirkwood

A Day With You

8/14/14 Age: 19

I patter across the kitchen,
Fixing myself breakfast in the quiet of the morning.
You're upstairs
Still asleep
After a late night
Of us talking.
Another long night where we talked about the world,
With so many wonderings, and so many questions,
Only to cross into lighter topics,
Becoming outrageously silly,
And laughing until we couldn't breathe.
Moments of quiet, solemn words,
Melting into talk of siblings,
Writing,
And our thoughts of the future,
Then slipping into making goofy faces,
Talking in silly voices,
And shaking with laughter –
A wild ride of conversation
Lasting late into the night.

I've been in your home so many times before,
It feels almost normal
Rummaging through your cupboards,
Getting myself breakfast.
Your father is the first person I see,
Whistling as he begins his day –
He smiles at me
Asking how I slept;
I answer and try to copy his whistled tune.

I see your mother not long later
And she wraps me in a hug –
For a few minutes we sit and talk
And she tells me funny stories
Of her childhood,
Or times when you were little.
Soon, you and your siblings are awake,
And we tease,
Chattering about random things,
Drifting crazily through
Our inside jokes,
And normal silliness.

The day goes on
And we amuse ourselves –
We share pictures,
While I take more.
We play with your pets,
And walk the horses over to pasture.
We reminisce about things we used to do
And teasingly argue
Over whose turn it is
To decide what we should do next.
Lunch passes
And supper comes –
We gather at the table
Holding hands while the blessing is said.
We pass around food
And talk about our day,
And the upcoming week,
Before the conversation drifts
Into the absurd teasing,
Lightheartedness
That I am so fond of.

Too many times
I almost choke
With the unfortunate mishap of laughing
While trying to swallow –
Coughing and giggling,
While you laugh too.
The day is flitting through my mind,
And for a moment I pause,
Smiling,
Realizing, as I look around fondly,
I feel so at home
Here
With you all.

Later in the evening
We gather in the living room
For a time of prayer and singing.
My heart feels full
As we worship
And thank God
For all our blessings;
As we bring Him
Our requests.
It is a time when it's safe to cry –
To openly take pleasure
In the rising praise of singing.
There's a feeling inside me
That I almost can't express –
Besides saying
It is a precious joy
To stand beside you all
And come before the Lord
Together.

When it's finally time to go
It's hard for me to leave.
Hugs are exchanged,
Goodbyes are said,
And I am told to invite myself over
Any time.
Oh, I know I'll be back
Very soon
To spend time with you again.

As I drive away
I feel a momentary war inside
To either laugh
Or cry
With the love that is in my heart.

What a blessing it is to be loved
And to know
That when I'm with you
It's home.

Colossians 3:12-13

"Put on then, as God's chosen ones, holy and beloved, compassionate hearts, kindness, humility, meekness, and patience, bearing with one another and, if one has a complaint against another, forgiving each other; as the Lord has forgiven you, so you also must forgive."

Sorry

5/15/10 Age: 15

There are thousands of words
That I wish I could take back;
Words that I said hastily, and judgment I did lack.
I said those things too quickly
When my temper was still hot;
Now that I am all alone, I wish that I had thought.
I didn't think at all when I said those words to you.
I quickly lost my temper, by anger was consumed.
I have asked God to forgive me,
But that can only be a start.
Now I have to tell you I am sorry from my heart.
So once again, I'm sorry;
I'll try to think things through.
Next time I get angry, I'll ask,
"What would Jesus do?"

Mark 11:25

"And whenever you stand praying, forgive, if you have anything against anyone, so that your Father also who is in heaven may forgive you your trespasses."

Please Forgive Me

8/14/14 Age: 19

The words I said were ugly –
I know they were unkind.
I never should have said them,
Or let them cross my mind.

The tone I used was hurtful.
I know that it was wrong.
My anger was a weapon –
A cruel and vicious prong.

The pain I gave was grievous.
I know I crossed the line.
I won't give you excuses,
For all those words of mine.

The way I spoke was sinful.
I know it wasn't fair.
I ask for your forgiveness
For speaking without care.

The fix won't be so easy –
I know I broke your trust.
I long to mend our friendship
In any way I must.

The truth is, I am sorry.
I hope you can forgive
The way I broke your trust today –
I pray our friendship lives.

Philippians 1:3-6

"I thank my God every time I remember you. In all my prayers for all of you, I always pray with joy because of your partnership in the gospel from the first day until now, being confident of this, that he who began a good work in you will carry it on to completion until the day of Christ Jesus."

Your Impact

8/25/14 Age: 19

I have a deep respect for you,
My friend.
There is a love
Pouring from your life
That ripples out in serving grace.
You've had times of sorrow
But still, it seems your love
Has only grown.
Your kindness is as evident
As a glowing light,
That makes me smile
Every time I think of you.
And that, friend,
Is a precious impact
You make on me.
Thank you.

I have a deep respect for you,
My friend.
There is a joy
Dancing around you,
Touching everyone you meet
With your delightful laughter.
You notice
The little things
That make people smile,
And share joyfulness
As easily as you breathe, it seems.
You've had your share of hard days,
But there are few people I know

Who are as genuinely joyful
As you.
And that, friend,
Is an encouraging impact
You make on me.
Thank you.

I have a deep respect for you,
My friend.
There is a hope
Echoing from your life
That fairly sings
Your love for our Savior.
When you speak of Him
And your longing to share His grace,
Tears often come to my eyes
At your passion.
You've reminded me so many times
To marvel at the wonderful knowledge
That Jesus knows the plans He has
For us.
You've had your times of questions,
Like any Christian does,
But again and again
You pour out the
Loving,
Joyful,
Hope-filled
Truth:
We can trust in God's goodness.
And that, friend,
Is the life-changing impact
You make on me...
Thank you.

"Please don't judge people by outward appearances. The most popular person I knew was the loneliest. The most jovial person I ever encountered was severely depressed. The people who I though had it all together were often hurting the worst. I've been thought arrogant when I was my most insecure. I've heard people say I was full of energy when I was my most exhausted. Truly, each heart knows it's own sorrow. You just never know what someone has been through, until you really, intimately get to know them."

~J. Grace Pennington,
author of
the **Firmament** series

Please Don't Judge The Outside

8/15/14 Age: 19

It's been a day of weariness –
Expectations take their toll,
As I am told I'm wonderful,
When I feel less than whole.

You say that I am popular –
Oh, look how I am loved!
Yet here I sit, the loneliest,
With dark emotions shoved.

You say that I'm respectable –
An example to the young.
But I am fighting battles
That you know nothing of.

You say I flow with tenderness –
There's such love in my stance.
But I keep pulling back away,
At every painful chance.

You say I have found joyfulness –
With smiles on my face.
But there is pain behind my eyes,
With no one to fill that space.

You say I show togetherness –
Life looks so figured out!
But I am warring with my past
And cringing in my doubt.

You say I'm almost arrogant –
My words seem backed by pride.
But really, I am insecure
And close myself inside.

You say there's boundless energy –
But that is not a fact.
For I am tired of this pace,
And weary of this act.

You speak of really knowing me –
And yet you never do.
You think I'm perfect at arm's length,
But I am broken too.

You speak still, almost glowingly,
Of all you see in me.
And yet I wish I trusted you,
To look and truly see.

"Remind your friend of things: Dreams they have for the future, exciting things they have planned, how much you care about them.
Now, I've discovered this completely from experience – when my friends remind me of these things, it makes me feel better inside. That's a problem with society nowadays, I think; people have stopped telling their friends or siblings what really matters. Take it from someone who's been at the bottom before –
sometimes, you just need to hear, 'I love you' or 'You're beautiful/amazing/wonderful' to keep going. Those words have come from my friends at some really dark times in my life, and they helped me to keep fighting."
~Theodora Ashcraft
author of the book
Of Whispers and Wanderings

What Should I Say?

3/30/13 Age: 18

What should I say
When my friend is in pain,
And they cry through the night,
And their world is insane?
Tell me, what should I say?

What should I say
When they can't fall asleep,
And the dark of their nightmares
Causes them to weep?
Tell me, what should I say?

What should I say
When they feel all alone,
And they ache deep inside –
Their heart sinks like a stone?
Tell me, what should I say?

What should I say,
When they lose someone dear,
And break down and cry,
And imagine in fear?
Tell me, what should I say?

What should I say
When they're used to a lie,
When they doubt their own worth,
And they wonder, "God why?"
Tell me, what should I say?

What should I say
When each day is a fight,
And they break in the dark,
And they're far from the light?
Tell me, what should I say?

Sometimes I say
Almost nothing at all,
Only, "I love you,
And I'll be here if you fall."
And then, I pray.

Sometimes I say,
That God is still here;
I remind them He's good,
And He sees the way clear.
And then, I pray.

For the things I say
Are only a seed.
And God is listening,
Providing words that I need.
He knows what to say.

"Know what we do when love hurts?
*We remember that it shows our love is **true**...*
*That our love is **real** and **deep** and **firm**...*
That it shows our love is not going through the
*motions, but that we **actually** care...*
And that sometimes,
that's what people need to know –
That we love them enough to love them,
though it aches.
***That** is what we remember when love hurts."*
~ZA

Loving Deep

12/22/13 Age: 18

Please someone,
Make it stop.
Pain curls its claws in my chest
All over again.
I'm sick from it...
But I won't give it up
By stepping back from those who cause
The hurt.
No,
I'll stand a little closer,
Open up a little wider,
And love a little deeper –
Until I'm dragged under the surface
In a wild instant of gut-wrenching sobs
And pain shrieking in mind–whirling
Emotion.
Curled up on the floor in my closet
Stifling the sound so no one will hear.
In bed with the covers over my head,
Gasping and shaking,
Praying and asking,
"God, *why*?"
Trembling, holding back the screams
I almost need to release.
Clenched fists, exhausting myself with the sobbing,
Yet, I can't stop.
Yes...
Some days, that is me:
Kneeling on the floor, arms clasped over my head,
Begging God to intervene...

Knowing that He can, and pleading with Him
To heal and grant peace...
Begging Him to take the pain away...
Yes, that is me.
Most days, it's less drastic –
A silent heaviness in my heart
Wishing I could do more,
Comforting with words that sound hollow
Even to me.
Too small,
Too empty...
What can I do to help?
I feel the need to shut down,
Distract myself,
While trying to bring comfort at the same time.
"I love you."
"I'm here."
"Forever."
"I promise."
Sinking myself deep,
Knowing the consequences
Of fully submerging my soul in your pain,
Of letting a piece of it
Become mine.
But I'm doing it anyway.
Letting tears slip by sometimes,
While praying.
Other times, too numb and shut in
To do anything but ache
And pray.
Please someone,
Make it stop.

But no, I can't let anyone stop it,
For to stop it would mean I stopped caring
And I won't do that.
Pain drives deep, but love goes deeper still –
Farther than the heartache,
And as the other half to the pain,
Reminding me that I break because I truly care,
In my own confusing way.
And this love?
This love is a bare, broken reflection of God's love,
A love that holds tight
In the midst of His children's sorrow.
The kind of love that cherishes you,
Though it knows there will be pain involved.
The kind of love that seeks out hope,
When life seems dreary and dark.
The kind of love that keeps close
Through all the blackest moments.
So here I am,
Small, weak, imperfect,
But I want you to know,
By God's strength and grace
I love you
With all my heart.

"Friendship is one of the sweetest joys of life. Many might have failed beneath the bitterness of their trial had they not found a friend."
~Charles H. Spurgeon

Friendship's Honesty

11/21/13 Age:18

Friendship's honesty is costly;
I'm afraid what you may see.
For you stepped behind the surface
To a deeper part of me.

Friendship's honesty is costly;
It hurts to bare my soul.
To wonder if rejection
Will finally take its toll.

Friendship's honesty is costly;
It seems easier to hide.
To build up my protection
To cover jealousy and pride.

Friendship's honesty is costly;
You know now what is real.
You look beyond the surface
And see all that I feel.

Friendship's honesty is costly,
Like a weapon you could use.
To share my truest longings
Is a way that I might lose.

Friendship's honesty is costly;
Now you see my wars within.
I wonder how our friendship
Isn't feeble, cracked, and thin.

Friendship's honesty is costly;
You could crush me since you know.
But I trust you for a reason –
For you'll never strike that blow.

Friendship's honesty is costly;
Yet it shows a bond of strength.
My temptation is to hide it
But I won't keep you at arm's length.

Friendship's honesty is costly;
But it's a price I'm glad to pay.
I can trust you with my wonderings
And the fears I cry and pray.

Friendship's honesty is costly;
In most cases it's a must.
Though not everyone will see it,
Friend, you have earned my trust.

Romans 12:9 – 16

"Let love be genuine. Abhor what is evil; hold fast to what is good. Love one another with brotherly affection. Outdo one another in showing honor. Do not be slothful in zeal, be fervent in spirit, serve the Lord. Rejoice in hope, be patient in tribulation, be constant in prayer. Contribute to the needs of the saints and seek to show hospitality.

Bless those who persecute you; bless and do not curse them. Rejoice with those who rejoice, weep with those who weep. Live in harmony with one another. Do not be haughty, but associate with the lowly. Never be wise in your own sight."

Unashamed To Love

3/26/14 Age: 19

Unashamed to answer.
Unashamed to call.
Unashamed to give a hand,
And love the ones who fall.

Unashamed to listen.
Unashamed to care.
Unashamed to stand beside
And help by being there.

Unashamed to whisper.
Unashamed to shout.
Unashamed to tell the truth
And chase away the doubt.

Unashamed to follow.
Unashamed to lead.
Unashamed to lay me down,
To fight until I bleed.

Unashamed to tire.
Unashamed to cry.
Unashamed to bow my head
And pray God shows you why.

Unashamed to wonder.
Unashamed to break.
Unashamed to stumble
And give more than I take.

Unashamed to notice.
Unashamed to see.
Unashamed to touch your tears,
And hold you tight to me.

Unashamed to love you.
Unashamed to pray.
Unashamed to be a friend
And someone who will stay.

*"When something makes you happy, treasure it.
Don't hesitate to tell the people you love
what they mean to you. Don't assume things will
stay the same – but don't let that make you afraid.
Let that knowledge fill you with passion to care...
If your moments are to become memories,
make them worth remembering.
If you are to become a memory to someone,
may that memory point to Jesus."*
~ZA

Loving And Being Loved

8/30/14 Age: 19

There is something so precious
In loving
And being loved –
Holding
And being held –
Caring
And being cared for –
Trusting
And being trusted –
Giving
And being given to –
Praying
And being prayed for –
That is friendship...
Friendship is love
In one of its truest forms.
Deep friendship says,
"I see you
And I'm letting myself be seen
As I am."
It says,
"I know you struggle –
I do too –
Let's walk this life together
To carry each other's burden
And encourage each other
Along the way."
It says,
"Let us rejoice together,
Cry together,

Live in harmony
And learn to forgive."
It says,
"I want to pour my life into yours;
Thank you
For being a part of mine."
When you see that love
Hold on tight
And cherish every moment of the blessing
God has given you
In that friendship.

"Real friendship, in an unconditional and eternal form, is the greatest gift you can expect to receive from anyone."
~Daniel Woltanski

"That's the thing with friends and friendship –
True friendship: It prevails, it fights back, it hurts, it breaks, it mends, it fails, it helps, it hopes.
It is exuberant happiness, it is the hardest pain, it is tenacity, it is love.
Sometimes we have to work through tough, messy situations; sometimes we have to be willing to be hurt and be willing to be vulnerable.
A friend is someone you like to hang out with, a best friend is someone who'll help you grow.
We're meant to be messes with other people so we can help each other through."
~Faith Marie Woltanski

Someone To Grow With

8/28/14 Age:19

A friend is someone to cry with
When life is filled with pain.
A friend is someone to hold to
When hope feels all in vain.

A friend is someone to pray with
When longings whisper, "Why?"
A friend is someone to ask with
When faith feels all but dry.

A friend is someone to sit with
As worries melt away.
A friend is someone to wait with
At the end of another day.

A friend is someone to laugh with
When times are long and drear.
A friend is someone to dance with
Full of joy at being near.

A friend is someone to learn with
With every year that's passed.
A friend is someone to find with
And pray these memories last.

A friend is someone to walk with –
To stand along beside.
A friend is someone to run with,
To reach for love inside.

A friend is someone to dream with –
To toss away the doubts.
A friend is someone to reach with,
With laughing, singing shouts.

A friend is someone to sing with,
With worship to our King.
A friend is someone to praise with,
For death has lost its sting.

A friend is someone to grow with,
To reach new heights untold.
A friend is someone to change with –
Watch every day unfold.

A Final Note:

This book's poems are very blatantly me, but not all of them are situations I've been in. Many are either built on emotion and imagination, or truth laced with stories... Heh, but many are fully my life, and situations as I've grown through the years.

Friendship has taught me a lot. Sometimes I've had to learn the hard way. Many times I have been blessed beyond measure with friendships I'd never have expected. It's been an interesting last few years, and I'm glad I've had friends to walk them with me.

I've been praying over this book:

I hope you are reminded you're not alone. I hope you perhaps see yourself somewhere here. I hope you find encouragement and peace in remembering – both the good and painful. I hope you consider your friendships, and how to be a good friend to those in your life. I hope you learn to give God your friendships – He loves them better than you ever can. He is the *Best Friend*.

Please remember:
Your friendships matter.
Don't shy away from true, deep friendship.
We are not meant to live life alone.
Friendship is a beautiful gift from God –
Yes, it can be messy, but it is worth it.

May God bless you and keep You in His grace.

~Ophelia – Marie Flowers

About The Author

I'm a homeschool graduate and full-time certified nurse aide who does a little writing on the side. I enjoy reading long Fantasy books, hanging out with my friends, teasing conversations, and living this life to the best of my abilities for God. Life has crazy bits, but it is so Beautiful in Christ.

If you'd like to contact me, you may email me at ophelia-writer@hotmail.com

Or visit my blogs:

za-blogging.blogspot.com
&
in-which-i-talk.blogspot.com

I would love to hear from you!

~Ophelia – Marie Flowers
Zeal Aspiring

ZAT

Made in the USA
Middletown, DE
20 March 2016